THE
LITTLE BOOK OF
WHISKEY

THE LITTLE
BOOK
OF
WHISKEY

SIP, EAT, DRINK

LYNDA BALSLEV

Andrews McMeel
PUBLISHING®

"CIVILIZATION BEGINS WITH DISTILLATION."

William Faulkner

AUTHOR

CONTENTS

"I WISH TO LIVE
TO 150 YEARS OLD,
BUT THE DAY I DIE,
I WISH IT TO BE
WITH A CIGARETTE
IN ONE HAND
AND A GLASS
OF WHISKEY IN
THE OTHER."

Ava Gardner

ACTRESS AND SINGER

"NEVER
CRY OVER
SPILT MILK.
IT COULD'VE
BEEN WHISKEY."

Bret (Pappy) Maverick

MAVERICK (1957)

INTRODUCTION

"WHAT WHISKEY
WILL NOT CURE, THERE
IS NO CURE FOR."

Irish proverb

Whiskey: It's not just your Dad's drink. Women and men of all ages are exploring and imbibing whiskey. State-of-the-art distilleries, whiskey bars, whiskey tastings, and food pairings are increasingly common, and with them come a growing curiosity and interest in learning more about this spirit made from distilled malted grains.

Whiskey's flavors and blends are numerous and nuanced, with hints of spice, caramel, coffee, vanilla, and smoke. These characteristics not only add complexity to each snifter sip, they lend depth and flavor to food—either as an accompaniment or a recipe ingredient.

Whether you drink whiskey or cook with it, this book provides a spirited introduction to the "water of life," with tips on how to drink, entertain, and cook with whiskey, including twenty-five recipes for sweet and savory dishes, as well as creative beverages and cocktails.

"COURAGE IS
A VITAMIN BEST
SWALLOWED
WITH WHISKEY."

Jarod Kintz

AUTHOR

ORIGIN AND
HISTORY

A MURKY PAST

"SOME OF YOU SAY
THAT RELIGION MAKES
PEOPLE HAPPY–
SO DOES WHISKY."

AMERICAN LAWYER

The word "whiskey" derives from the Irish or Gaelic words *uisce beatha* or *uisge-beatha*, which are translations of the Latin term *aqua vitae* or "water of life," meant to describe spirits.

The origin of whiskey is somewhat murky. It's agreed that whiskey originated in the British Isles, yet, depending on which side of the Irish sea you sit, there are differing opinions (best discussed over a dram) as to whether the precise origin was in Ireland or Scotland.

For the record, whiskey distillation can be traced as far back as the fifteenth century. The Irish monks are often credited with introducing the technique of distillation from their travels in the Middle East during the Middle Ages, where they witnessed grape distillation; and the barber surgeons, who worked in the Irish monasteries, distilled spirit alcohol for medicinal purposes. The Irish will tell you that following the dissolution of their monasteries in the sixteenth century, the newly independent monks introduced whiskey-making to the Scottish Highlands and shared their distilling craft. Meanwhile, the Scots, with their own faithful take on the origin, might argue that whiskey distillation naturally evolved on their home turf from their abundance of barley grain.

As for the first distilleries, the Old Bushmills Distillery, in what is now Northern Ireland, began manufacturing whiskey in 1608, and Ireland's Kilbeggan Distillery was established in 1757 as the first licensed distillery in the British Isles. From that point on, distilleries were born on both sides of the Irish Sea.

WHAT IS
WHISKEY?

(THERE'S NO SUCH THING
AS A STUPID QUESTION)

"WHISKY IS
LIQUID SUNSHINE."

George Bernard Shaw

IRISH PLAYWRIGHT

Whiskey is a distilled alcoholic beverage made from fermented grain mash, which is essentially a weak beer. Different grains can be used to make whiskey, including barley, corn, rye, and wheat, and the amounts and choice of grains reflect and define the provenance and type of whiskey. For instance, Scotch whisky is predominantly made of malted (germinated) barley, while corn is the dominant grain in bourbon, and rye is the dominant grain (surprise) in American rye.

MALTING

Whiskey begins as a grain, often barley, that contains starch that needs to be turned into soluble sugars to make alcohol. Malting is the process of soaking the grain for two to three days and then allowing the moist grain to slightly germinate, which converts the starch to sugar. Once the grain shoots, the process is stopped by drying it in a kiln. The grain is now "malt," which is ground down.

MASHING

The ground-down grain (or grist) is added to water to extract the soluble sugars before fermentation. The combination of malt and water is called "mash." The mash is agitated in a large tank to dissolve and extract the sugars, which are drained off, and this liquid is called the "wort."

Note that the source of the water will influence the flavor of the final spirit, with varying minerals and pH levels, so location plays a distinguishing key in whiskey character. For instance, Kentucky bourbon whiskey is made with limestone-filtered spring water, which is naturally purified and mineral-rich, with elevated pH levels. Scotch whisky sources its water from lochs, rivers, and springs, with varying mineral and pH levels, and the source's proximity to the sea can add brininess to the flavor.

FERMENTATION

The wort is passed into a tank, where yeast strains are introduced to begin fermentation, which is the conversion of sugars to alcohol. The process takes about forty-eight hours, resulting in a low-alcohol liquid similar to beer, aptly called "distiller's beer," which is then distilled.

DISTILLATION

Distillation is the process of heating a liquid and creating a vapor, which is captured and condensed into another liquid. This method is done with pot or column stills. Pot stills are usually made of copper and, as the name implies, shaped like a spherical pot, and they operate on a batch-by-batch basis, which is best suited for smaller production. Pot stills are the earliest design, having evolved from the ancient alembic, which was used for alcoholic distillation as far back as the ninth century. Column stills, also known as Coffey stills, were developed later in the nineteenth century. They are sleek and industrial, and can be made of copper, stainless steel, or a combination of the two. Column stills operate continuously, so they are better suited for larger-scale production.

The number of distillations varies based on the whiskey and the producer. For example, Scotch whisky is usually distilled twice, while Irish whiskey is usually distilled three times. With each round of distillation, the whiskey becomes more pure and smooth.

MATURATION

Once the liquid is distilled, the spirit is put into wood (often oak) barrels to age.

The nature of the barrel—such as the source of the wood and whether the cask has been formerly used to mature other types of spirits, such as sherry, port, or rum—will influence the color, aroma, and flavor of the whiskey. The spirit is left to mature in warehouses for a minimum of two to three years (depending on the whiskey) and up to twelve, fifteen, or even thirty years.

"MY MAMA ALWAYS TOLD ME THERE ARE FEW THINGS A GOOD HUG CAN'T CURE, AND THOSE THINGS ARE WHAT BOURBON'S FOR."

J. T. Geissinger

AUTHOR

YOU SAY
WHISKEY
I SAY
BOURBON

WHAT'S THE DIFFERENCE?

"THERE IS NO BAD WHISKEY.
THERE ARE ONLY SOME
WHISKEYS THAT AREN'T
AS GOOD AS OTHERS."

Raymond Chandler

AMERICAN-BRITISH NOVELIST
AND SCREENWRITER

Simply put, the differences between whiskeys are geography, spelling, and ingredients. Whiskey is the overarching term (and the general term used in this book), while Scotch whisky (without an "e") is made in Scotland, and bourbon whiskey is made in the United States.

Scotch whisky is distilled from malted barley, which is often dried over peat smoke, lending Scotch its coveted smoky flavor. Scotch whisky is usually distilled twice and aged in former bourbon, sherry, or port casks for a minimum of three years. Popular brand examples include: Ballantine's, Chivas Regal, Cutty Sark, Dewar's, Glenfiddich, and Johnnie Walker.

Irish whiskey, with an "e," is distilled from a mix of malted and unmalted barley, which is kiln-dried and rarely peated; therefore it lacks a smoky character and tastes more like the grain. Irish whiskey is often triple distilled, which yields a smoother sip, and aged in new or former bourbon, sherry, or rum casks for a minimum of three years. Popular brand examples include: Bushmills, Jameson, Powers, Redbreast, Teeling, and Tullamore D.E.W.

Bourbon whiskey is distilled from a mix of grains with a minimum of fifty-one percent corn, which makes it a sweeter spirit with an appealing vanilla-caramel flavor. Bourbon must be aged in charred, new-oak barrels for at least two years. Popular brand examples include: Buffalo Trace, Elijah Craig, Four Roses, Jim Beam, Maker's Mark, and Wild Turkey.

American rye whiskey is made from a blend of grains with a minimum of fifty-one percent rye (instead of corn), which makes it drier and spicier than bourbon. Like bourbon, it must be aged in charred, new-oak barrels for at least two years. Popular brands include: Bulleit, Michter's, Old Overholt, Rittenhouse, Sazerac, and Templeton.

Tennessee whiskey is made the same way as bourbon, as both are distilled from at least fifty-one percent corn and go into charred new-oak barrels to age. The difference is that before the distilled clear spirit is put into the barrels, Tennessee whiskey is first filtered through or steeped in charcoal. This filtering process reduces harsh flavors and results in a smoother whiskey. Popular brands include: Corsair, Jack Daniel's, George Dickel, Nelson's Green Brier, Pritchard's, and Rollins.

Canadian whisky is often labeled rye whisky (no "e"); however, unlike American rye, it does not require fifty-one percent rye and is often a blend of rye and corn. It's smoother and milder, with the grains fermented, distilled, and aged separately before blending. Popular brands include: Canadian Club, Collingwood, Crown Royal, Forty Creek, Pendleton, and WhistlePig.

Japanese whisky is often made in the style of Scotch (from malted barley, peated and twice distilled) but without the restraint of long-established traditions. Therefore, the range of styles, blends, and profiles are left to the whim of the producer, with variances that invite tasting. Popular brands include: Nikka, Suntory, and Togouchi.

"WHISKEY, LIKE
A BEAUTIFUL
WOMAN, DEMANDS
APPRECIATION.
YOU GAZE FIRST,
THEN IT'S TIME
TO DRINK."

Haruki Murakami

JAPANESE AUTHOR

SNIFF
AND
SIP

HOW TO DRINK WHISKEY

"THE LIGHT MUSIC OF
WHISKEY FALLING INTO
A GLASS—AN AGREEABLE
INTERLUDE."

James Joyce
AUTHOR

WHICH GLASS?

For all whiskeys, the glasses
are ideally bulbous with a
narrow rim to capture the
aroma of the spirit. A short
and sturdy Glencairn glass
is a popular alternative
to a long-stem glass, and
more stable (which is
useful when drinking
spirits!). For purists, the
advantage of a long-stem tulip
glass is that it separates the
hand and nose, preventing

any aromas from the hand from interfering with the whiskey aroma. A rocks or old-fashioned glass is ideal for most cocktails. While its wide rim is less conducive to nosing, it's a more versatile glass. This is the best choice for all occasions, especially if you are seeking an all-purpose drinking glass.

SNIFF AND SIP

Hold the glass below your nose and sniff (unlike wine, do not swirl and do not insert your nose into the glass). Open your mouth a little and breathe again. Pay attention to the aroma—is it smoky, spicy, fruity?

Take a small sip and hold it on your tongue while you breathe through your nose. Swallow and breathe through your mouth. Pay attention to the flavors in your mouth, on your tongue, and in the back of your throat. How does the flavor change? Is it sweet or spicy, herbal or medicinal, sharp or mellow? How does it finish when you swallow?

WATER OR ICE?

After the initial taste, add a few drops of water to the whiskey and taste again. A small splash of water opens up the flavor of the whiskey by slightly reducing the alcohol content. Use still spring water if possible, since treated tap water may spoil the flavor. Avoid ice, as the chill will dull the flavor of the whiskey.

"YOU SAY TOMATO, I SAY BOURBON AND COKE."

Drew Carey

ACTOR

"IF I CANNOT
DRINK BOURBON
AND SMOKE CIGARS
IN HEAVEN, THEN
I SHALL NOT GO."

Mark Twain

AUTHOR

PARTY

HOW TO HOST
A WHISKEY TASTING

"SLEEP LATE, HAVE FUN,
GET WILD, DRINK WHISKEY,
AND DRIVE FAST ON
EMPTY STREETS WITH
NOTHING IN MIND BUT
FALLING IN LOVE AND NOT
GETTING ARRESTED."

Hunter S. Thompson

AMERICAN JOURNALIST AND AUTHOR

Hosting a whiskey tasting party is a fun way to gather friends with a shared interest in whiskey. There are many ways to host a party. To get started, here are a few steps to follow as a general guide.

FORMAT

Choose the number of guests to invite. Six to eight guests is a good number. It's just enough to provide a reasonable whiskey selection without being a crowd. Keep in mind that a twenty-five ounce (750 mL) bottle of whiskey serves twelve people a two-ounce pour each. For tastings, you may want to pour more conservatively. The good news is that there will be leftovers, which you can keep or give to your guests to take home as party favors.

You can offer a vertical tasting where just one category of whiskey is selected. For instance, host a bourbon tasting, an Irish whiskey tasting, or a Scotch tasting. Alternatively, you can choose to offer a horizontal tasting where a single bottle from multiple categories is presented, such as one each of bourbon, Tennessee whiskey, rye, Scotch, and Irish whiskey. Keep the horizontal selections in a similar price range for comparison, but try to avoid bottom-shelf spirits, as they are less for tasting than for mixing.

Choose five bottles on average, so as not to overwhelm the taste buds. While you can gallantly purchase the bottles yourself, it can easily add up. To spread the love, ask each guest to bring a bottle according to the theme. Then they can bring home the leftovers.

Lay out the flavors found in whiskey for aroma reference, such as coffee beans, dark chocolate, vanilla beans, peaches, sherry, and honey.

Provide pens and paper for tasting notes. Provide a little background on each whiskey. You can do this yourself or task your guests to describe the whiskey they provide.

Provide still spring water at room temperature to clean the palate between tastes, and a bucket for pouring out tasters, if desired.

Offer simple neutral tasting nibbles, such as bread or water crackers, to help absorb the alcohol without competing with the flavor of the whiskey.

METHOD

Begin the tasting order with smooth and soft whiskeys, and save the strongest (highest-proof) and the smokiest peated whiskeys for last.

Sniff each whiskey and pay attention to the aromas; for instance, are they spicy, smoky, woody, fruity?

Pour the tastings neat (no water, no ice) at first, and follow with a splash of water (if desired) to open up the flavor, then make a note of the difference in each type.

Refer to tasting flavors, such as: vanilla, dark chocolate, toffee, maple, brown sugar, tropical, seaweed, briny, malt, biscuit, wheat, straw, dried fruit, apricot, apple pie, sweet, honey, cinnamon, or nutmeg.

Record the aromas and tasting notes for each whiskey, both for your reference and to share with the guests.

APRÈS TASTING

Plan a meal following the tasting to extend the evening and absorb the alcohol.

Share the leftover bottles with your guests as party favors.

It's advised not to let anyone drive home. Have a designated driver or use a ride-share.

"ALWAYS CARRY A FLAGON OF WHISKEY IN CASE OF SNAKEBITE AND FURTHERMORE, ALWAYS CARRY A SMALL SNAKE."

W.C. Fields

ACTOR AND COMEDIAN

"TOO MUCH
OF ANYTHING
IS BAD, BUT
TOO MUCH
GOOD WHISKEY
IS BARELY
ENOUGH."

Mark Twain

AUTHOR

THE PROOF IS IN THE

PUDDING

COOKING AND PAIRING FOOD WITH WHISKEY

"HAPPINESS IS HAVING
A RARE STEAK, A BOTTLE
OF WHISKY, AND A DOG
TO EAT THE RARE STEAK."

Johnny Carson

LATE-NIGHT TELEVISION HOST

Whiskey, like salt, is a flavor enhancer in cooking. During cooking, the evaporation of the alcohol concentrates the flavor characteristics of the whiskey while coaxing out similar flavor characteristics in the food.

Flavors such as wheat, malt, and peaty smokiness, as well as vanilla, toffee, and caramelized sugars from barrel aging bring out similar flavor notes in food. For example, a peated Scotch will emphasize smoked food, such as salmon and mackerel. A honeyed whiskey or sweet bourbon complements game meats, chocolate, fruit, jams, and caramel. A spicy, fruity rye whiskey will enhance unctuous meat, such as pork and lamb, as well as sharp cheeses, chutneys, and tangy fruits like apples.

When cooking with whiskeys, as with wine, choose a whiskey you would like to drink; however, save your priciest bottles for sipping. A simple solution is to purchase miniature (50 mL) bottles of your spirit of choice for cooking.

Pay attention when cooking with whiskey. High-alcohol spirits can easily ignite. Never add the alcohol directly from the bottle to a pan over a flame. Pour the liquid into a measuring cup, remove the pan from the heat, and add the alcohol.

When pairing food with whiskey, follow

the same matching principles as with cooking and choose a whiskey with a similar flavor profile. Single out a flavor in the whiskey to highlight, such as smoke, dried fruit, or chocolate. For lighter dishes like seafood, choose a lighter, lower-proof whiskey, and for richer, more robust dishes like steak, choose a bolder whiskey with a higher proof.

RECIPES

"WHISKEY IS BY
FAR THE MOST
POPULAR OF
ALL REMEDIES
THAT WON'T
CURE A COLD."

Jerry Vale

SINGER

APPETIZERS AND SIDES

SPICED BOURBON PECANS
44

WHISKY–CARAMELIZED ONION SOUP AU GRATIN
46

ROASTED CARROT AND BOURBON SOUP
50

MAPLE BACON–BOURBON GLAZED HASSELBACK SWEET POTATOES
53

FARROTTO SALAD WITH DELICATA SQUASH, DRIED CRANBERRIES, AND WHISKEY BALSAMIC GLAZE
56

SPICED BOURBON PECANS

MAKES 2 CUPS

Bourbon's sweet vanilla and caramel notes, tinged with a touch of earthiness, naturally meld with buttery-rich pecans, which explains why these two ingredients have a natural affinity.

This recipe makes a great appetizer or packaged gift. Choose a sweet, nutty bourbon, such as Maker's Mark.

½ CUP PACKED LIGHT BROWN SUGAR

¼ CUP BOURBON WHISKEY

1 TEASPOON SEA SALT

1 TEASPOON GROUND CUMIN

½ TEASPOON GROUND CINNAMON

½ TEASPOON CAYENNE

2 CUPS PECAN HALVES

1 Preheat the oven to 325°F. Line a rimmed baking sheet with parchment paper.

2 Combine the sugar, bourbon, salt, cumin, cinnamon, and cayenne in a medium bowl, and whisk to blend. Add the pecans, and stir to thoroughly coat.

3 Pour the pecans onto the prepared baking sheet and spread them out in one layer. Bake until browned and crusty, 18 to 20 minutes, stirring once or twice during cooking. Remove from the oven, and slide the parchment paper and pecans onto a rack to cool completely. Break the pecans apart and store in an airtight container for up to 1 week.

WHISKY–CARAMELIZED ONION SOUP AU GRATIN

SERVES 4

Whisky and beer partner up in this warming soup, which puts a Scottish twist on the classic French onion. Be patient with the onions—the long cooking time is essential for extracting their sweet flavor and browning. Consider the time spent as an opportunity to pour a dram of whisky for yourself and relax in front of a fire before the soup is ready.

Choose a fruity, peated Scotch whisky, such as Johnnie Walker.

2 TABLESPOONS UNSALTED BUTTER

1 TABLESPOON EXTRA-VIRGIN OLIVE OIL

3 POUNDS YELLOW ONIONS (ABOUT 5 LARGE),
HALVED LENGTHWISE AND THINLY SLICED

SEA SALT

1 CLOVE GARLIC, MINCED

½ CUP SCOTCH WHISKY

3 TABLESPOONS ALL-PURPOSE FLOUR

1 CUP PALE ALE

4 CUPS ORGANIC BEEF STOCK (OR MUSHROOM
STOCK FOR VEGETARIAN OPTION)

FRESHLY GROUND BLACK PEPPER

4 SLICES COUNTRY-STYLE BREAD, ¾-INCH THICK

1½ CUPS GRATED GRUYÈRE AND/OR EMMENTAL
CHEESE

CONTINUED

1 Melt the butter with the oil in a large Dutch oven or soup pot over medium heat. Add the onions and ½ teaspoon of salt. Cook until the onions soften and are golden brown and slightly caramelized, or about 40 minutes, stirring occasionally. Add the garlic and stir until fragrant, or about 30 seconds. Pour in the whisky and continue to cook until nearly evaporated, 1 to 2 minutes, stirring constantly.

2 Whisk in the flour and cook until the onions darken slightly, or about 2 minutes. Add the ale, bring to a boil, and cook until the liquid is reduced by about half, 2 to 3 minutes. Add the stock, 1 teaspoon of salt, and ½ teaspoon of black pepper. Simmer, partially covered, for 20 minutes. Taste for seasoning.

3 While the soup is cooking, prepare the bread. Preheat the oven to 350°F. Arrange the bread on a baking sheet and bake for 15 minutes. Turn off the oven without removing the bread to let the bread crisp.

4 When the soup is ready, remove the bread from the oven and heat the oven broiler. Ladle the soup into four oven-proof bowls or crocks placed on a baking sheet. Arrange a bread slice over each bowl and spread the cheese over the bread. Broil until the cheese is melted and bubbly, 2 to 3 minutes. Serve immediately.

ROASTED CARROT
AND BOURBON SOUP

SERVES 3 TO 4

This bourbon-laced soup is earthy and spicy with the warming fragrance of whiskey. Cut the carrots on the diagonal so that more of their surface area will brown while roasting; the char and the carrots' natural sweetness will complement the sweet caramel notes of bourbon. Choose a bourbon with vanilla and woody char notes, such as Jim Beam.

1 POUND CARROTS, PEELED AND SLICED ON THE DIAGONAL, ¼-INCH THICK

2 TABLESPOONS EXTRA-VIRGIN OLIVE OIL, DIVIDED

SEA SALT

1 SMALL YELLOW ONION, FINELY CHOPPED (ABOUT ½ CUP)

⅓ CUP BOURBON WHISKEY

3 CUPS CHICKEN BROTH

½ TEASPOON DRIED THYME

¼ TEASPOON FRESHLY GROUND BLACK PEPPER

¼ TEASPOON CAYENNE

FRESH THYME LEAVES, FOR GARNISH

1 Preheat the oven to 400°F. Combine the carrots, 1 tablespoon of oil, and ½ teaspoon of salt in a medium bowl, and toss to coat. Spread the carrots in one layer on a rimmed baking sheet and roast in the oven until tender and golden brown on the bottom, or about 15 to 20 minutes.

CONTINUED

2 Heat 1 tablespoon of oil in a large saucepan over medium heat. Add the onions and sauté until translucent, or about 3 minutes. Carefully pour in the bourbon and cook until the bourbon is reduced to about 1 tablespoon, 1 to 2 minutes. Add the carrots, chicken broth, thyme, ½ teaspoon of salt, black pepper, and cayenne. Bring to a boil, decrease the heat to low, and cover. Simmer until the carrots are very tender, or about 30 minutes. Remove from the heat, uncover, and cool for 10 minutes.

3 Carefully transfer the soup, in batches, to a food processor or blender, and process or blend until smooth. Return the soup to the pot. Add ½ cup of water and reheat over medium-low heat. If a thinner soup is desired, add 1 to 2 more tablespoons of water. Serve warm, garnished with fresh thyme leaves.

MAPLE BACON–BOURBON GLAZED HASSELBACK SWEET POTATOES

SERVES 4

Sweet bourbon and maple are a perfect flavor match. Team them up with salty bacon and luscious sweet potatoes, and you will have a side dish that will vie for center stage. Hasselback potatoes are a fun and pretty way to serve spuds and sweet potatoes. When thinly sliced in an accordion pattern, the tiny ridges crisp while letting the basting juices drizzle into the potato flesh. Slice the potatoes nearly to the bottom without piercing so that the potatoes remain intact. Choose a smoky bourbon with maple notes, such as Elijah Craig.

CONTINUED

4 MEDIUM SWEET POTATOES

4 SLICES THICK-CUT BACON

¼ CUP MAPLE SYRUP

2 TABLESPOONS BOURBON WHISKEY

½ TEASPOON SEA SALT

¼ TEASPOON FRESHLY GROUND BLACK PEPPER

SOUR CREAM

CHOPPED FRESH CILANTRO

1 Cut the potatoes crosswise in thin slices, about ⅛-inch thick, ¾ of the way through the potatoes, without piercing the bottoms.

2 Preheat the oven to 375°F.

3 Cook the bacon in a skillet over medium heat until crisp, or about 6 minutes. Transfer to a plate lined with a paper towel to cool.

4 Pour off all but 2 tablespoons of fat from the skillet. Add the maple syrup, bourbon, salt, and pepper, and whisk over medium-low heat to dissolve the sugar.

5 Place the potatoes in a baking dish. Brush the potatoes all over with the glaze, making sure to get in the crevices. Bake until tender and beginning to crisp, or about 45 minutes, depending on the size of the potatoes.

6 Spoon a dollop of sour cream over each potato. Crumble the bacon over the tops, and garnish with the cilantro. Serve warm.

FARROTTO SALAD WITH DELICATA SQUASH, DRIED CRANBERRIES, AND WHISKEY BALSAMIC GLAZE

SERVES 4 TO 6

When you switch out the rice in risotto with farro grains, you have farrotto. The difference with farro is that it doesn't demand the constant stirring required by Arborio rice. The sturdy farro grains hold their shape while cooking, so you can leave them to soak up the simmering liquid, which in this case includes a blast of whiskey, a robust complement to the earthy farro. The whiskey adds a sweet kick of flavor to the grains as well as the glaze that lacquers the squash. This colorful salad may be served as a vegetarian main dish or a rustic side. Choose a bright, robust whiskey with sherry notes, such as Bushmills Black Bush.

FARRO

1 TABLESPOON UNSALTED BUTTER

1 TABLESPOON EXTRA-VIRGIN OLIVE OIL

1 CUP SEMI-PEARLED FARRO, RINSED

¼ CUP WHISKEY

2 CUPS CHICKEN STOCK (OR MUSHROOM STOCK
   FOR VEGETARIAN OPTION)

½ TEASPOON SEA SALT

GLAZE

¼ CUP BALSAMIC VINEGAR

¼ CUP WHISKEY OR BOURBON

2 TABLESPOONS LIGHT BROWN SUGAR

1 CLOVE GARLIC, SMASHED BUT INTACT

½ CUP EXTRA-VIRGIN OLIVE OIL

¼ TEASPOON SEA SALT

¼ TEASPOON FRESHLY GROUND BLACK PEPPER

2 SMALL DELICATA SQUASH, SEEDED AND
   SLICED CROSSWISE INTO ¼-INCH SLICES

4 OUNCES ARUGULA

⅓ CUP DRIED CRANBERRIES, DIVIDED

2 TABLESPOONS PEPITAS (PUMPKIN SEEDS)

CONTINUED

1 To cook the farro, melt the butter with the olive oil in a small saucepan over medium heat. Add the farro and cook, stirring constantly, until lightly toasted, or about 1 minute. Add the whiskey and simmer until nearly evaporated, or about 1 minute. Add the stock and salt, partially cover the pot, and cook until the farro is tender and the liquid is absorbed, or about 30 minutes. Cool to room temperature.

2 To make the glaze/dressing, combine the balsamic vinegar, whiskey, brown sugar, and garlic in a small saucepan. Bring to a boil over medium heat and reduce the liquid by about half, or about 8 minutes. Cool to room temperature and discard the garlic. Add the oil, salt, and black pepper, and whisk to emulsify.

3 To prepare the squash, preheat the oven to 375°F. Arrange the squash on a rimmed baking sheet and lightly brush with the glaze. (Reserve the remaining glaze to dress the salad.) Roast the squash until tender and golden brown in spots, or about 25 minutes.

4 To assemble, scatter the arugula on a large serving platter or shallow bowl. Sprinkle the farro over and around the arugula and scatter half of the cranberries over the salad. Top with the squash slices. Drizzle the remaining glaze over the salad, and garnish with the remaining cranberries and the pepitas.

"I SIPPED MY SCOTCH.
IT WAS SMOKY AND
SMOOTH, TASTING
OF PEAT AND AGED
OAK, UNDERSCORED
BY LICORICE AND THE
INTANGIBLE ESSENCE OF
SCOTTISH MASCULINITY.
I LIKED MY SCOTCH
UNDILUTED, LIKE I
LIKED MY TRUTH."

Viet Thanh Nguyen

AUTHOR

MAIN DISHES

WHISKEY–SPIKED CHEESE FONDUE
62

WHISKEY BEEF STEW
66

**WHISKY–GLAZED BURGERS
WITH CHEESE AND BACON**
70

BOURBON–GLAZED BABY BACK RIBS
74

**STICKY BOURBON–GINGER
CHICKEN THIGHS**
77

WHISKEY–GLAZED CHILE SHRIMP
80

SCOTCH–CURED SALMON
83

WHISKEY–SPIKED CHEESE FONDUE

SERVES 6

Cheese fondue traditionally relies on a kick of spirit to fortify the pot of cheese and cut its creamy richness. While the Swiss use fruity kirsch, this recipe looks to the British Isles for inspiration. A glug of honeyed Irish whiskey lends necessary sweet and sharp notes to the cheese, which is a blend of sharp and piquant cheddar and Gruyère. Choose a clean, fruity Irish whiskey, such as Tullamore D.E.W.

¼ CUP IRISH WHISKEY

3 TABLESPOONS CORNSTARCH

½ TEASPOON SALT

½ TEASPOON FRESHLY GROUND BLACK PEPPER,
   PLUS EXTRA FOR SERVING

¼ TEASPOON GROUND NUTMEG

3 CUPS DRY WHITE WINE

1 LARGE CLOVE GARLIC, MINCED

1 POUND COARSELY GRATED GRUYÈRE CHEESE

8 OUNCES GRATED SHARP CHEDDAR CHEESE

1 LOAF COUNTRY-STYLE OR LEVAIN BREAD, CUT
   INTO ¾-INCH CUBES

PARBOILED VEGETABLES, SUCH AS SMALL
   POTATOES, CAULIFLOWER, AND BROCCOLI
   FLORETS, FOR DIPPING

Note: Have all of your ingredients ready before you begin. Once you start, the fondue will come together quickly and must be constantly stirred. The fondue must not come to a boil.

CONTINUED

1 Whisk the whiskey, cornstarch, salt, black pepper, and nutmeg in a small bowl until smooth. Set aside.

2 Combine the wine and garlic in a large, heavy saucepan or fondue pot. Heat over medium heat until tiny bubbles form, giving the wine a fizzy appearance without coming to a boil. Add the cheese one handful at a time, stirring constantly, until each handful is melted before adding the next—do not let the fondue boil.

3 Once all the cheese is added, continue stirring for 1 to 2 minutes to slightly thicken—do not let the fondue boil.

4 Stir in the cornstarch mixture and continue to stir until the mixture thickens to a fondue consistency. (Some cornstarch brands thicken more easily than others. If your fondue remains thin, whisk 1 more tablespoon of cornstarch with 2 tablespoons of white wine, and stir into the cheese.)

5 When the fondue is ready, remove from the heat. Pour the cheese into a warm fondue pot if necessary and place over a fondue burner. Serve immediately with the bread and vegetables for dipping.

WHISKEY BEEF STEW

SERVES 4 TO 6

This hearty no-nonsense stew is a must for a cold winter night. It isn't fancy, but it is delicious, comforting, and ensures warmth with a bracing boost of whiskey in the stock. Scotch, rye, or Irish whiskey are all suitable contenders—just remember to pour yourself a glass to sip while you pass the time and the stew simmers. As with many rich soups and stews, the flavors will develop when left overnight in the refrigerator.

2½ POUNDS BEEF CHUCK, EXCESS FAT TRIMMED AND CUT INTO 1-INCH PIECES

SALT

FRESHLY GROUND BLACK PEPPER

3 TABLESPOONS EXTRA-VIRGIN OLIVE OIL, DIVIDED

1 MEDIUM YELLOW ONION, CHOPPED

8 OUNCES WHITE MUSHROOMS, HALVED (QUARTERED IF LARGE)

2 MEDIUM CARROTS, PEELED AND SLICED ¼-INCH THICK

3 CLOVES GARLIC, CHOPPED

½ CUP WHISKEY

3 TABLESPOONS TOMATO PASTE

1 TEASPOON DRIED THYME

4 CUPS BEEF STOCK

1 BAY LEAF

1 TABLESPOONS DARK BROWN SUGAR

CONTINUED

1 Preheat the oven to 325°F. Season the beef with salt and pepper.

2 Heat 1 tablespoon of oil in a Dutch oven over medium-high heat. Add the beef (in batches) in one layer, without overcrowding, and brown on all sides. Transfer the meat to a plate and repeat with the remaining beef.

3 Pour off all but 1 tablespoon of fat from the Dutch oven. Add the onion and sauté until softened, or about 2 minutes. Add the mushrooms and sauté until softened, or about 2 minutes. Add the carrots and garlic, and sauté until the carrots brighten in color and the garlic is fragrant, or about 2 minutes. Pour the whiskey into the pot and deglaze, scraping up any brown bits with a spoon. When the whiskey has reduced by about half, add

the tomato paste and thyme, and cook, stirring
constantly, about 1 minute. Return the beef
to the pot and add the stock, bay leaf, sugar,
1 teaspoon of salt, and ½ teaspoon of black
pepper. The meat should be just covered
with liquid. If not, add additional stock until
covered. Bring to a boil, then cover the pot and
transfer to the oven. Cook until the meat is
tender, or about 2 hours, stirring occasionally.

4 Serve warm, ladled into bowls.

WHISKY–GLAZED BURGERS WITH CHEESE AND BACON

SERVES 4

These stacked burgers are doubly spiked with a whisky glaze, which is both mixed into the meat patties and brushed on them while grilling. The extra boost adds another layer of spice, fruit, and, in the case of Scotch, smoke to these double-fisted burgers topped with crispy bacon, cheddar, and fresh salad fixings. Choose a spiced, fruity Scotch, such as Cutty Sark.

2 TABLESPOONS SCOTCH WHISKY

2 TABLESPOONS WORCESTERSHIRE SAUCE

1 TEASPOON DIJON MUSTARD

1 TEASPOON GRANULATED GARLIC

½ TEASPOON SEA SALT

¼ TEASPOON FRESHLY GROUND BLACK PEPPER

1½ POUNDS GROUND BEEF

4 SLICES SHARP CHEDDAR CHEESE (ABOUT 4 OUNCES)

4 HAMBURGER BUNS, SLICED

4 THICK-CUT BACON SLICES, COOKED UNTIL CRISP AND HALVED CROSS-WISE

LETTUCE LEAVES

TOMATO SLICES

RED ONION SLICES

CONTINUED

1 Whisk the whisky, Worcestershire sauce, mustard, garlic, salt, and pepper in a small bowl. Combine 3 tablespoons of the glaze and the beef in a bowl and mix to combine.

2 Form the meat into 4 patties and make an indentation in the center of each patty with your thumb (this will prevent the burgers from puffing up on the grill).

3 Prepare the grill for direct cooking over medium heat.

4 Grill the patties until cooked to your desired doneness, 8 to 10 minutes for medium-rare, flipping once and basting once or twice with the glaze during cooking.

- 2 POUNDS RIPE PEACHES, PITTED AND SLICED ¼-INCH THICK; OR 2 (10-OUNCE) PACKAGES FROZEN PEACH SLICES
- ½ CUP PACKED LIGHT BROWN SUGAR
- ¼ CUP BOURBON WHISKEY
- 2 TABLESPOONS FRESHLY SQUEEZED LEMON JUICE
- 2 TEASPOONS FINELY GRATED, FRESHLY-PEELED GINGER
- 1 CINNAMON STICK
- 1 TEASPOON FINELY GRATED LEMON ZEST
- 1 TEASPOON VANILLA EXTRACT
- PINCH OF SEA SALT

Combine all the ingredients in a large saucepan. Bring to a simmer over medium heat, stirring to dissolve the sugar. Decrease the heat to medium-low and simmer, uncovered, until slightly thickened and the peaches are soft but not mushy, 15 to 20 minutes. Remove from the heat and cool to room temperature; discard the cinnamon stick. Store, covered, in the refrigerator for up to 1 week.

SCOTCH APPLE CRISP

SERVES 6 TO 8

Homey apple crisp is elevated with an infusion of whisky in the crisp and the addition of Salted Whisky Caramel Sauce (page 94). The sauce is a keeper, so make a double batch and serve it drizzled over ice cream or your favorite desserts. Choose a fruity Scotch whisky, such as Cutty Sark.

TOPPING

1½ CUPS ALL-PURPOSE FLOUR

½ CUP PACKED LIGHT BROWN SUGAR

¼ CUP GRANULATED SUGAR

1 TEASPOON GROUND CINNAMON

¼ TEASPOON SALT

½ CUP WALNUTS (OPTIONAL)

¾ CUP UNSALTED BUTTER, CHILLED AND CUT
   IN PIECES

FILLING

2½ POUNDS GRANNY SMITH APPLES, PEELED,
   CORED, AND CUT IN ¾-INCH CHUNKS

⅓ CUP GRANULATED SUGAR

2 TABLESPOONS SCOTCH WHISKY

1 TABLESPOON FRESHLY SQUEEZED ORANGE
   JUICE

1 TABLESPOON ALL-PURPOSE FLOUR

1 TEASPOON FINELY GRATED ORANGE ZEST

½ TEASPOON GROUND CINNAMON

½ TEASPOON GROUND NUTMEG

CONTINUED

1 To make the topping, combine the flour, sugars, cinnamon, and salt in the bowl of a food processor. Pulse once or twice to combine. Add the walnuts, if using, and pulse a few times to break them into coarse pieces. Add the butter, and pulse until the topping resembles a coarse meal. (The topping may be made up to 1 day in advance. Cover and refrigerate until use.)

2 To make the filling, preheat the oven to 375°F. Put the apples in a large bowl. Whisk the sugar, whisky, orange juice, flour, zest, cinnamon, and nutmeg in a small bowl, pour over the apples, and toss to coat. Transfer the apples to an 8 by 10-inch gratin dish. Spread the topping over the apples.

3 Bake in the oven until the topping is golden brown and the fruit is bubbling, or about 50 minutes. Remove from the oven and cool slightly (or to room temperature) before serving. Serve with vanilla ice cream or whipped cream, and drizzle with Salted Whisky Caramel Sauce (page 94).

SALTED WHISKY CARAMEL SAUCE

This is a luscious sauce for the dessert repertoire. It's delicious and decadent when drizzled over pies, cakes, and ice cream (or simply licked from the spoon)—consider making a double batch to compensate for any spoon-licking.

1 CUP GRANULATED SUGAR

6 TABLESPOONS UNSALTED BUTTER, ROOM TEMPERATURE AND CUT IN PIECES

½ CUP HEAVY CREAM

2 TABLESPOONS SCOTCH WHISKY, SUCH AS CUTTY SARK

½ TEASPOON SEA SALT

Cook the sugar in a medium saucepan over medium heat, without stirring, until it begins to melt. When it's nearly melted, continue to cook, stirring occasionally, until the sugar thoroughly melts and turns amber in color, 6 to 7 minutes. Add the butter carefully (it may splatter) and stir until smooth. Remove from the heat, and whisk in the cream, whisky, and salt until smooth. Cool slightly and pour into a glass jar that has a lid. Cool completely, uncovered. Serve, or cover and refrigerate for up to 1 month.

BOURBON–SPIKED CARROT CAKE WITH CREAM CHEESE FROSTING

SERVES 12

This is a light and moist sheet cake, fragrant with spice and the whiff of bourbon. While the bourbon isn't pronounced, it melds beautifully with the raisins and spices and deepens the flavor of this rich cake. Choose a well-rounded bourbon with brown sugar, vanilla, and caramel flavors, such as Evan Williams.

CAKE

1 CUP GOLDEN RAISINS

½ CUP BOURBON WHISKEY

2 CUPS ALL-PURPOSE FLOUR

2 TEASPOONS GROUND CINNAMON

1½ TEASPOONS BAKING POWDER

1 TEASPOON BAKING SODA

½ TEASPOON SALT

½ TEASPOON ALLSPICE

½ TEASPOON GROUND NUTMEG

¼ TEASPOON GROUND CLOVES

4 LARGE EGGS

1 CUP VEGETABLE OIL

1 CUP PACKED DARK BROWN SUGAR

½ CUP GRANULATED SUGAR

2 TEASPOONS FINELY GRATED ORANGE ZEST

1 TEASPOON VANILLA EXTRACT

2 CUPS PACKED, PEELED, AND GRATED CARROTS

1 CUP CHOPPED PECANS OR WALNUTS

CONTINUED

FROSTING

1 (8-OUNCE) PACKAGE CREAM CHEESE, SOFTENED

½ CUP UNSALTED BUTTER, SOFTENED

1 TABLESPOON BOURBON WHISKEY

½ TEASPOON VANILLA EXTRACT

2 TO 3 CUPS SIFTED CONFECTIONERS' SUGAR

1 To make the cake, combine the raisins and bourbon in a small saucepan. Bring to a boil over medium heat and immediately remove from the heat. Let stand for 30 minutes.

2 Preheat the oven to 350°F. Grease an 8 by 11-inch baking pan and line with parchment paper.

3 Combine the flour, cinnamon, baking powder, baking soda, salt, allspice, nutmeg, and cloves in a medium bowl, and stir to blend.

4 Combine the eggs, oil, sugars, orange zest, and vanilla in the bowl of an electric mixer, and mix on medium speed for 1 minute. Add the flour mixture and mix on low speed to just combine, without overmixing. Stir in the raisins, bourbon, carrots, and nuts.

5 Pour the batter into the prepared pan and spread evenly. Bake until a toothpick inserted in the center comes out clean, or about 40 minutes. (If the top starts to darken before the cake is thoroughly cooked, lightly cover with foil.) Transfer to a rack and cool completely.

CONTINUED

6 To prepare the frosting, cream together the cream cheese and butter in the bowl of an electric mixer until light and fluffy, or about 1 minute. Add the bourbon and vanilla, and mix to blend. Add the sugar, 1 cup at a time, until you have a thick frosting consistency, 2½ to 3 cups.

7 Invert the cooled cake on a platter. Spread or pipe the frosting over the top. Garnish with finely grated orange zest. Cut into squares to serve.

CHOCOLATE WHISKEY POUND CAKE WITH WHISKEY CREAM

MAKES 1 LARGE POUND CAKE OR BUNDT CAKE; SERVES 8 TO 10

This is a hefty cake not for the faint of heart. Irish whiskey and dark chocolate partner up in a rich and decidedly adult cake. You might think the whiskey cream is overdoing it, but the spirited dollop of airy cream adds the perfect touch to this dense and moist pound cake. Choose an Irish whiskey with vanilla notes, such as Bushmills Original.

CONTINUED

CAKE

1 CUP UNSALTED BUTTER, ROOM TEMPERATURE

½ CUP IRISH WHISKEY

6 OUNCES DARK CHOCOLATE (70%), FINELY CHOPPED

2 TABLESPOONS UNSWEETENED COCOA POWDER

1¾ CUPS ALL-PURPOSE FLOUR

1 TEASPOON BAKING POWDER

½ TEASPOON BAKING SODA

½ TEASPOON SALT

3 LARGE EGGS

¾ CUP PACKED DARK BROWN SUGAR

¾ CUP GRANULATED SUGAR

1 TEASPOON VANILLA EXTRACT

½ CUP SOUR CREAM

WHISKEY CREAM

1 CUP HEAVY CREAM

1 TABLESPOON GRANULATED SUGAR

2 TEASPOONS IRISH WHISKEY

½ TEASPOON VANILLA EXTRACT

1   To make the cake, preheat the oven to 350°F. Butter and line a 9 by 5-inch loaf pan with parchment paper. Butter the parchment paper. If using a Bundt pan, butter an 8-cup Bundt pan and skip the parchment paper.

2   Heat the butter and whiskey in a medium saucepan over medium-low heat until the butter melts, stirring occasionally. Remove the pan from the heat, add the dark chocolate and cocoa, and whisk until smooth.

3   Whisk the flour, baking powder, baking soda, and salt in a small bowl.

CONTINUED

4 Whisk the eggs and sugars in a large bowl until light and fluffy. Whisk in the chocolate and vanilla, then whisk in the sour cream until blended. Add the dry ingredients, and stir to combine without overmixing.

5 Pour the batter into the prepared pan. Place on a baking sheet and transfer to the oven. Bake until the cake is set and a toothpick inserted in the center of the cake comes out clean, 55 to 60 minutes. If the top is firm and beginning to crack before the center is fully cooked, loosely cover with foil. Transfer the cake to a rack and cool in the pan for 5 minutes. Turn the cake out onto the rack and cool completely.

6 Before serving, make the whipped cream. Beat the cream in the bowl of an electric mixer until traces of the whisk are visible. Add the sugar, whiskey, and vanilla, and continue to whip until soft peaks form. Cut the cake into serving pieces and serve with the whipped cream.

"LOVE MAKES
THE WORLD
GO 'ROUND?
NOT AT ALL.
WHISKEY MAKES
IT GO 'ROUND
TWICE AS FAST."

Compton Mackenzie

SCOTTISH AUTHOR

BEVERAGES AND COCKTAILS

SIMPLE SYRUP

MAKES 1 CUP

1 CUP GRANULATED SUGAR
1 CUP WATER

Heat the sugar and water in a small saucepan over medium heat until the sugar dissolves. Bring to a simmer and remove from the heat. Let cool to room temperature. The syrup may be stored in the refrigerator for up to 2 weeks.

GINGER SIMPLE SYRUP

MAKES 1 CUP

1 CUP GRANULATED SUGAR
1 CUP WATER
**4 OUNCES FRESH GINGER, PEELED AND THINLY
   SLICED**

Heat the sugar and water in a small saucepan
over medium heat until the sugar dissolves. Bring
to a simmer, then add the ginger. Remove from
the heat, cover, and let steep until it reaches room
temperature. Strain and discard the ginger. The
syrup may be stored in the refrigerator for up to 1
week.

SPICED BROWN SUGAR SYRUP

MAKES 1 CUP

1 CUP LIGHT BROWN SUGAR
1 CUP WATER
1 (2-INCH) CINNAMON STICK
4 WHOLE CLOVES
ZEST OF ½ ORANGE

Heat the sugar and water in a small saucepan over medium heat until the sugar dissolves. Bring to a simmer, then add the cinnamon, cloves, and orange zest. Remove from the heat, cover, and let steep until it reaches room temperature. Strain and discard the solids. The syrup may be stored in the refrigerator for up to 1 week.

HOT WHISKEY CIDER

SERVES 1

This fireside drink combines the makings of a hot toddy with hot-spiced cider, and once you've tried it, you'll agree it's a match made in heaven. Sweet bourbon or a honeyed Irish whiskey are best for this warming winter cocktail.

5 OUNCES APPLE CIDER

1 (2-INCH) CINNAMON STICK

4 WHOLE CLOVES

2 TEASPOONS HONEY

2 OUNCES IRISH WHISKEY OR BOURBON

ORANGE SLICE, FOR GARNISH

Heat the apple cider, cinnamon, and cloves in a small saucepan until hot. Decrease the heat to low and let steep for 10 minutes. Whisk in the honey, then add the whiskey. Remove from the heat and strain into a mug. Garnish with an orange slice.

WHISKEY AFFOGATO

SERVES 1

Affogato means "drowned" in Italian. In the case of this coffee drink, it refers to vanilla ice cream, which is "drowned" in a double shot of hot espresso. The heat of the espresso begins to melt the ice cream, turning this dessert into a luscious, creamy beverage. In this recipe, a bracing splash of your favorite whiskey is also added, which technically means the ice cream is drowned twice, so perhaps this adult treat should be called a Double Affogato.

2 SCOOPS OF YOUR FAVORITE HIGH-QUALITY VANILLA ICE CREAM (ABOUT ½ CUP)

2 OUNCES HOT ESPRESSO

1 OUNCE SCOTCH OR IRISH WHISKEY

Scoop the ice cream into a 6 to 8-ounce glass or small bowl. Pour the espresso over, then drizzle with the whiskey. Enjoy immediately.

MAPLE
OLD-FASHIONED

SERVES 1

It makes perfect sense to substitute maple syrup for the traditional sugar cube in an old-fashioned. The maple pairs beautifully with the orange and amplifies the vanilla, caramel, and maple notes in bourbon.

1 (2-INCH) ORANGE PEEL

2 TEASPOONS MAPLE SYRUP

1 TEASPOON WATER

2 TO 3 DASHES ANGOSTURA BITTERS

ICE CUBES

2 OUNCES BOURBON WHISKEY

MARASCHINO CHERRY, FOR GARNISH

Rub the orange peel around the rim of an old-fashioned glass. Add the maple syrup, water, and bitters, and stir to blend. Fill with ice and pour the bourbon over. Twist the peel and add to the drink. Garnish with a cherry, if desired.

IRISH MULE

SERVES 1

Whiskey lends an Irish lilt to the classic Moscow Mule. Add a few muddled leaves of fresh mint to the mix and this is one variation you will make again—and again. A good Mule is bright and fresh, so only use fresh lime juice (not a sugary mixer) and don't hold back on the mint.

6 FRESH MINT LEAVES

ICE CUBES

2 OUNCES IRISH WHISKEY

1 OUNCE FRESHLY SQUEEZED LIME JUICE

6 OUNCES GINGER BEER

LIME WEDGE

In a chilled copper mug, lightly muddle the mint leaves. Add 3 to 4 ice cubes, the whiskey, and the lime juice. Top off with the ginger beer. Serve with a lime wedge.

BOURBON MINT JULEP

SERVES 1

This southern cocktail is the equivalent of an adult slushie. The mint should not be overly muddled, so instead of muddling the leaves with sugar, simple syrup is added with the bourbon. Ginger Simple Syrup may be substituted for the Simple Syrup. It's not traditional, but for those who are less inclined to take the classic route, it adds a little kick to a hot and sultry day. Horse race viewing is entirely optional.

6 TO 8 LARGE MINT LEAVES, PLUS A MINT SPRIG FOR GARNISH

2 OUNCES BOURBON WHISKEY

½ OUNCE SIMPLE SYRUP (PAGE 109) OR GINGER SIMPLE SYRUP (PAGE 110)

CRUSHED ICE

In a double old-fashioned glass or a 10-ounce glass, lightly muddle the mint to bruise and release the oil from the leaves. Add the bourbon and Simple Syrup, and fill the glass with crushed ice. Stir to blend and chill the glass. Top with more crushed ice and garnish with a mint sprig.

JOHN COLLINS

SERVES 1

John Collins is essentially a whiskey sour cocktail—or, better yet, an adult lemonade. It's similar to a Tom Collins, but it includes whiskey instead of gin. A dry, spicy rye or smooth, sweet bourbon are both good options for this refreshing cocktail.

2 OUNCES RYE OR BOURBON WHISKEY

1 OUNCE FRESHLY SQUEEZED LEMON JUICE

½ OUNCE SIMPLE SYRUP (PAGE 109)

ICE CUBES

2 OUNCES SPARKLING WATER

LEMON SLICE, FOR GARNISH

Combine the whiskey, lemon juice, and syrup
in a cocktail shaker. Add ice, cover, and shake
until chilled. Pour into a 10-ounce Collins glass
filled with ice, and top with the sparkling water.
Garnish with a lemon slice.

SAZERAC

SERVES 1

Hold on to your hats. This quintessential New Orleans spin on a classic whiskey cocktail is notably enhanced by the absinthe rimming the glass. If you are feeling exceptionally festive, pour the swirled absinthe into the cocktail before serving.

1 TEASPOON GRANULATED SUGAR (OR 1 SUGAR CUBE)

1 TEASPOON WATER

3 DASHES PEYCHAUD'S BITTERS

2 DASHES ANGOSTURA BITTERS

ICE CUBES

2½ OUNCES RYE WHISKEY

2 TEASPOONS ABSINTHE

TWIST OF LEMON PEEL

1 Muddle the sugar, water, and bitters in a chilled mixing glass to dissolve the sugar. Add the rye and fill with ice. Stir until chilled, 20 to 30 seconds.

2 Pour the absinthe into a chilled old-fashioned glass and swirl to coat. Pour out the excess and reserve, if desired. Fill the glass with ice. Strain the cocktail into the prepared glass and add the reserved absinthe, if using. Garnish with a twist of lemon peel.

POMEGRANATE WHISKEY COCKTAIL

SERVES 1

This light and refreshing cocktail is brightened with lemon and pomegranate juice and a dash of floral Peychaud's Bitters. It's also dangerously easy to sip. Use a fruity, spicy rye or bourbon for this sweet and tart cocktail, such as Rittenhouse rye or Four Roses bourbon.

2 OUNCES RYE OR BOURBON WHISKEY

½ OUNCE COINTREAU

2 OUNCES FRESHLY SQUEEZED LEMON JUICE

2 OUNCES POMEGRANATE JUICE

2 TEASPOONS GINGER SIMPLE SYRUP
(PAGE 110)

2 DASHES PEYCHAUD'S BITTERS

ICE CUBES

1 HEAPING TEASPOON POMEGRANATE ARILS
(SEEDS)

ORANGE SLICE, FOR GARNISH

Combine the whiskey, Cointreau, lemon juice, pomegranate juice, syrup, and bitters in a chilled old-fashioned glass filled with ice, and stir. Garnish with the pomegranate arils and orange slice.

BOURBON PUNCH WITH ORANGES AND CRANBERRIES

SERVES 13 TO 15

Break out the punch bowl and make this colorful punch the centerpiece of your next holiday party. Orange and Christmas spice make everything nice in this winter-season punch spiked with bourbon. Use freshly squeezed orange juice for best results. Choose a reasonably priced fruity, vanilla bourbon, such as Maker's Mark.

1 (750 ML) BOTTLE BOURBON WHISKEY

2 CUPS CRANBERRY JUICE

2 CUPS FRESHLY SQUEEZED ORANGE JUICE

1 CUP SPICED BROWN SUGAR SYRUP (PAGE 111)

2 TO 3 CUPS COLD SELTZER WATER

4 TO 5 CUPS ICE CUBES

2 NAVEL ORANGES, SLICED

1 CUP WHOLE FRESH CRANBERRIES

1 Combine the bourbon, cranberry juice, orange juice, and syrup in a large pitcher or bowl, and refrigerate for at least 2 hours.

2 To serve, pour into a punch bowl. Add 2 cups of seltzer water and taste; add up to 1 more cup of seltzer water, if desired. Add the ice, and garnish with the orange slices and fresh cranberries. Serve in glasses with ice.

"A GOOD GULP OF HOT WHISKEY AT BEDTIME— IT'S NOT VERY SCIENTIFIC, BUT IT HELPS."

Alexander Fleming

SCOTTISH MICROBIOLOGIST

"I SHOULD
NEVER HAVE
SWITCHED
FROM SCOTCH
TO MARTINIS."

Humphrey Bogart

ACTOR

METRIC CONVERSIONS AND EQUIVALENTS

APPROXIMATE METRIC EQUIVALENTS

Volume

¼ teaspoon	1 milliliter
½ teaspoon	2.5 milliliters
¾ teaspoon	4 milliliters
1 teaspoon	5 milliliters
1¼ teaspoons	6 milliliters
1½ teaspoons	7.5 milliliters
1¾ teaspoons	8.5 milliliters
2 teaspoons	10 milliliters
1 tablespoon (½ fluid ounce)	15 milliliters
2 tablespoons (1 fluid ounce)	30 milliliters
¼ cup	60 milliliters
⅓ cup	80 milliliters
½ cup (4 fluid ounces)	120 milliliters
⅔ cup	160 milliliters
¾ cup	180 milliliters
1 cup (8 fluid ounces)	240 milliliters
1¼ cups	300 milliliters
1½ cups (12 fluid ounces)	360 milliliters
1⅔ cups	400 milliliters
2 cups (1 pint)	480 milliliters
3 cups	720 milliliters
4 cups (1 quart)	0.96 liter
1 quart plus ¼ cup	1 liter
4 quarts (1 gallon)	3.8 liters

Mass

¼ ounce	7 grams
½ ounce	14 grams
¾ ounce	21 grams
1 ounce	28 grams
1¼ ounces	35 grams
1½ ounces	42.5 grams
1⅔ ounces	47 grams
2 ounces	57 grams
3 ounces	85 grams
4 ounces (¼ pound)	113 grams
5 ounces	142 grams
6 ounces	170 grams
7 ounces	198 grams
8 ounces (½ pound)	227 grams
16 ounces (1 pound)	454 grams
35.25 ounces (2.2 pounds)	1 kilogram

Length

⅛ inch	3 millimeters
¼ inch	6.25 millimeters
½ inch	1.25 centimeters
1 inch	2.5 centimeters
2 inches	5 centimeters
2½ inches	6.25 centimeters
4 inches	10 centimeters
5 inches	12.75 centimeters
6 inches	15.25 centimeters
12 inches (1 foot)	30.5 centimeters

METRIC CONVERSION FORMULAS

To Convert	Multiply
Ounces to grams	Ounces by 28.35
Pounds to kilograms	Pounds by .454
Teaspoons to milliliters	Teaspoons by 4.93
Tablespoons to milliliters	Tablespoons by 14.79
Fluid ounces to milliliters	Fluid ounces by 29.57
Cups to milliliters	Cups by 240
Cups to liters	Cups by .236
Pints to liters	Pints by .473
Quarts to liters	Quarts by .946
Gallons to liters	Gallons by 3.785
Inches to centimeters	Inches by 2.54

OVEN TEMPERATURES

To convert Fahrenheit to Celsius, subtract 32 from Fahrenheit, multiply the result by 5, then divide by 9.

Description	Fahrenheit	Celsius	British Gas Mark
Very cool	200°	95°	0
Very cool	225°	110°	¼
Very cool	250°	120°	½
Cool	275°	135°	1
Cool	300°	150°	2
Warm	325°	165°	3
Moderate	350°	175°	4
Moderately hot	375°	190°	5
Fairly hot	400°	200°	6
Hot	425°	220°	7
Very hot	450°	230°	8
Very hot	475°	245°	9

COMMON INGREDIENTS AND THEIR APPROXIMATE EQUIVALENTS

1 cup uncooked white rice = 185 grams
1 cup all-purpose flour = 120 grams
1 stick butter (4 ounces • ½ cup • 8 tablespoons) = 110 grams
1 cup butter (8 ounces • 2 sticks • 16 tablespoons) = 220 grams
1 cup brown sugar, firmly packed = 213 grams
1 cup granulated sugar = 200 grams

Information compiled from a variety of sources, including *Recipes into Type* by Joan Whitman and Dolores Simon (Newton, MA: Biscuit Books, 1993); *The New Food Lover's Companion* by Sharon Tyler Herbst (Hauppauge, NY: Barron's, 2013); and *Rosemary Brown's Big Kitchen Instruction Book* (Kansas City, MO: Andrews McMeel, 1998).

ABOUT THE AUTHOR

Lynda Balslev is an award-winning cookbook author and food and drinks writer who is passionate about sharing her knowledge through the lens of travel and culture. Lynda is the author of six books, including *Almonds: Recipes, History, Culture* and *The Little Book of Fika*. She currently writes a nationally syndicated food column and blog: *TasteFood.* Her work has appeared in various print and digital media, including NPR, Culture, Parade, Relish, and Marin Magazine.

Andrews McMeel Publishing
a division of Andrews McMeel Universal
1130 Walnut Street, Kansas City, Missouri 64106

www.andrewsmcmeel.com

22 23 24 25 26 SHO 10 9 8 7 6

ISBN: 978-1-5248-5099-9

Library of Congress Control Number: 2019940390

Editor: Jean Z. Lucas
Art Director/Designer: Holly Swayne
Illustrations: Sierra Stanton
Production Editor: Margaret Daniels
Production Manager: Carol Coe